Abish and the Queen

written by Tiffany Thomas
illustrated by Nikki Casassa

CFI · An imprint of Cedar Fort, Inc. · Springville, Utah

HARD WORDS:
Abish, queen, servant, angry

PARENT TIP: Have a special celebration
the first time a child reads an entire book
without help.

This is Abish.
She is the
queen's servant.

Ammon tells King Lamoni
how to be good.

King Lamoni falls down.
The people think he is dead.

The queen asks Ammon.
Ammon says the king is not dead.

The queen believes Ammon.
The king wakes up.

The king teaches the queen.
They both fall down.

Abish tells all the people.
She believes Ammon.

The people
are angry
at Ammon.
Abish cries.

Abish holds the queen's hand.
She wakes up.

The queen holds the king's hand.
He wakes up.

They are all
good now.

The end.

ISBN 13: 978-1-4621-4337-5

Published by CFI, an imprint of Cedar Fort, Inc. • 2373 W. 700 S., Suite 100, Springville, UT 84663
Distributed by Cedar Fort, Inc., www.cedarfort.com

Cover design and interior layout design by Shawnda T. Craig
Cover design © 2022 Cedar Fort, Inc.
Printed in China • Printed on acid-free paper
10 9 8 7 6 5 4 3 2 1